AMISH PRAYERS

AMISH PRAYERS

Compiled by

BEVERLY
LEWIS

Published by Bethany House Publishers
11400 Hampshire Avenue South
Bloomington, MN 55438
www.bethanyhouse.com

Bethany House Publishers is a division of
Baker Publishing Group, Grand Rapids, Michigan.

Printed in the United States of America

In keeping with biblical principles of creation stewardship, Baker Publishing Group advocates the responsible use of our natural resources. As a member of the Green Press Initiative, our company uses recycled paper when possible. The text paper of this book is comprised of 30% post-consumer waste.

Library of Congress Cataloging-in-Publication Data

Ernsthafte Christenpflicht. English Selections.
    Amish prayers : heartfelt expressions of humility, gratitude, and
       devotion / compiled by Beverly Lewis.
    p. cm.
    "Translation from Die Ernsthafte Christenpflicht prepared by Katie
       Polley"—T.p. verso.
ISBN 978-0-7642-0882-9 (hardcover : alk. paper)
1. Prayers. I. Lewis, Beverly, 1949– II. Polley, Katie. III. Title.
BV260.E7613 1997
242'.80973—dc22

2010051456

Das Vaterunser

Unser Vater in dem Himmel!
    Dein Name werde geheiligt.
Dein Reich komme. Dein Wille geschehe auf Erden
    wie im Himmel.
Unser täglich Brot gib uns heute.
Und vergib uns unsere Schuld,
    wie wir unseren Schuldigern vergeben.
Und führe uns nicht in Versuchung, sondern erlöse uns von
dem Übel. Denn dein ist das Reich und die Kraft und die
Herrlichkeit in Ewigkeit. Amen.

Matthaeus 6:9–13, LUTH1545

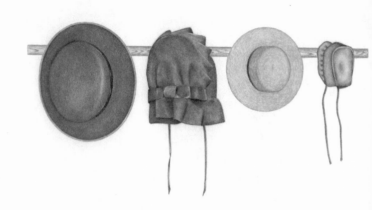

Contents

Foreword

The German prayer book *Die Ernsthafte Christenpflicht* has held a dear place in the hearts of Anabaptists since the date of its earliest printing in 1708. Immigrant Anabaptists committed many of the original long prayers to memory and read them to their children each morning and evening. Along with the old German Bible, the written prayers were regarded as a precious possession, and today they continue to be embraced by Amish and Mennonites alike.

The excerpts of prayers included in this new edition have been translated afresh from the original German prayer book, which has remained unchanged since its first printing.

While compiling the sometimes beseeching, often

praise-filled prayers found here, I sensed a deep spiritual connection to the European Christians who first penned these earnest petitions to our heavenly Father. Because some of my own ancestors on my paternal great-grandmother's side were persecuted and martyred for the sake of Christ in the year 1685, I am profoundly honored and most humbled to be connected in any small way to this revered collection.

My Swiss ancestors brought copies of the *Christenpflict* to the New World, where they settled and farmed a two-thousand-acre tract of land (originally purchased from William Penn) that later came to be called Paradise in Lancaster County, Pennsylvania. It was there that both my maternal grandparents, Omar and Ada Buchwalter, were born. Their parents' farmland adjoined, and Omar and Ada learned as little children to pray the Lord's Prayer, as well as a few of the prayers printed in this book.

Each prayer and accompanying Scripture passage can be used either in personal devotions or collectively with fellow worshippers. My Plain friends and relatives in Pennsylvania, Ohio, and Indiana use the prayers in their morning and evening family worship, as silent table prayers, and in private quiet time. Several prayers are read publicly after the testimonies are given during Amish house-church and other Sunday gatherings, or are shared in smaller group settings.

It is my hope that divine comfort and inspiration might spring from these remarkable Christian prayers, perhaps as a tool for confessing sin, offering thanksgiving, or guiding one's worship. Most of all, I pray that you, the reader, might grasp some measure of the original writers' desire for peace and protection in the midst of shared danger, as well as a fervent longing to embrace the grace and mercy of God while living in obedience to Christ's teachings.

Beverly Lewis

Prayers
for a New Day

LORD, ALMIGHTY GOD AND HEAVENLY
Father, you did not give us life and set us
in this world merely so we would nourish ourselves with
grief and work until we return to the dust from whence
we came. Instead, you ordained our lives so that we
should fear you and love you, and cleave to you with all
our hearts. Even as your divine grace gave us the day to
work, so you gave us the night to rest. Under your fatherly
shield of protection, we have mercifully enjoyed this rest,
and for that we humbly praise and bless you with deep
gratitude. Amen.

TO EVERY THING THERE IS A SEASON, AND A TIME
TO EVERY PURPOSE UNDER THE HEAVEN.

Ecclesiastes 3:1

YOU HAVE ONCE AGAIN LET DAY DAWN FOR us, O heavenly Father; may we remember this is your merciful gift. Teach us to understand why you have given us this glorious gift, and why you let your wonderful sun rise above us: so we may live each day according to your will and prepare ourselves for the never-ending day you will create.

Holy Father, may we learn to abandon and avoid the night of darkness and sin so we may walk in the clear light of your divine mercy. Let us set aside the acts of darkness and take up the weapons of light so that we may always walk with integrity. Amen.

FOR THE LORD GOD IS A SUN AND SHIELD:
THE LORD WILL GIVE GRACE AND GLORY:
NO GOOD THING WILL HE WITHHOLD
FROM THEM THAT WALK UPRIGHTLY.

Psalm 84:11

A S YOU HAVE LOVED US, HOLY FATHER, SO may we obey you out of childlike love; just as we acknowledge your fatherly love, so may we love our neighbors as ourselves. Let us do nothing contrary to this love, and so do right by our neighbors.

We ask, holy Father, that we may enjoy in moderation all you give us to fulfill our needs and not misuse it due to extravagance or evil impulses. Give us a sensible heart, one faithful with your gifts and not overly concerned for food, drink, or earthly nourishment. Instead, teach us to put our faith in you and to yearn for your divine help and grace. Give us a humble, broken spirit, a penitent nature, true gentleness, and a hunger and thirst for your righteousness. Amen.

AND BE YE KIND ONE TO ANOTHER,
TENDERHEARTED, FORGIVING ONE ANOTHER,
EVEN AS GOD FOR CHRIST'S SAKE
HATH FORGIVEN YOU.

Ephesians 4:32

IVE US THIS DAY A HEART THAT IS PURE in your sight, O Lord, so we might look upon you. O God and Father of love and peace, grant us your eternal peace and grace so we may at all times prove ourselves peace-loving people and avoid all evil discord and strife. May we endure with a meek spirit and calm heart any hardship we encounter on this earth, be it a cross or tribulations, disgrace, or merely misfortune. Since you are our God and Creator, O Lord, reconcile our life and walk with your holy and divine will, for all our works and deeds are in your hands. We commend ourselves and our families, body and soul, into your care, Lord. Govern and promote our work, O God, according to your will. Amen.

BE YE HOLY; FOR I AM HOLY.

1 Peter 1:16

MAY YOUR MERCIFUL EYES BE ON US DAY and night, O Lord. Cover us with your divine protection and shield. Judge, rule, and bless all of our undertakings for your glory. Amen.

THE LORD IS MY STRENGTH AND MY SHIELD;
MY HEART TRUSTED IN HIM, AND I AM HELPED:
THEREFORE MY HEART GREATLY REJOICETH; AND
WITH MY SONG WILL I PRAISE HIM.

Psalm 28:7

O LORD OUR GOD, YOU GENTLY SHED heaven's light upon us to enlighten us. Merciful Father, you grant us each day so we may use it according to your holy will and blessing.

For these your gracious gifts, we give you praise, honor, and thanks, O holy Father. We ask you, dear Father, to forgive our sins against you today and all our trespasses against your divine will; we confess in repentance and sorrow the sins we have committed through idleness and negligence. Forgive us for the sake of your dear Son, Jesus Christ, in whose name we ask to be reconciled to you. May we now and forevermore be at peace with you through your Son, O holy Father. Amen.

FOR HE HATH MADE HIM TO BE SIN FOR US, WHO
KNEW NO SIN; THAT WE MIGHT BE MADE THE
RIGHTEOUSNESS OF GOD IN HIM.

2 Corinthians 5:21

YOU ARE OUR CREATOR AND PROVIDER, O Lord and heavenly Father, under whose gracious protection we have mercifully passed this night in peaceful rest. For this we praise and thank you! But, dear Father, where we have in some way abused your kindness against your divine will, we freely confess and ask that you would forgive us for the sake of your dear Son, Jesus Christ. Amen.

BUT NOW THUS SAITH THE LORD THAT CREATED
THEE . . . FEAR NOT: FOR I HAVE REDEEMED THEE,
I HAVE CALLED THEE BY THY NAME;
THOU ART MINE.

Isaiah 43:1

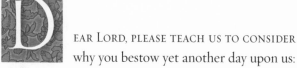

DEAR LORD, PLEASE TEACH US TO CONSIDER why you bestow yet another day upon us: so that we may spend the rest of our days in a sober, just, and godly way; so that your holy name is honored and praised; and so that we may forever remain in your grace and become holy. From now on, may your Spirit lead us, and may your angels bless our path. O God, we ask this in the name of your beloved Son, Jesus Christ. Amen.

I WILL LEAD THEM IN PATHS THAT THEY
HAVE NOT KNOWN: I WILL MAKE DARKNESS
LIGHT BEFORE THEM.

Isaiah 42:16

O MERCIFUL, GRACIOUS GOD, FATHER OF eternal light and comfort, whose goodness and faithfulness are fresh again each morning, we give you praise, honor, and thanks for the lovely daylight, and also for graciously protecting us during the night and granting us gentle sleep and rest. May we now arise in your grace and love, and under your care and protection, make gainful, joyful use of the daylight. Amen.

EVERY GOOD GIFT AND EVERY PERFECT GIFT
IS FROM ABOVE, AND COMETH DOWN FROM
THE FATHER OF LIGHTS, WITH WHOM IS NO
VARIABLENESS, NEITHER SHADOW OF TURNING.

James 1:17

HEAVENLY FATHER, ABOVE ALL THINGS enlighten us with the eternal light that is our Lord Jesus Christ so that His mercy and knowledge may shine in us. Preserve the light of faith in our hearts, multiply it, and strengthen it. Awaken your love in us, confirm our hope, and give us true humility so we may walk in the footsteps of Jesus. Let a reverence for you be in all our deeds and before our eyes. Drive all spiritual darkness and blindness from our hearts. Protect us today and always from superstition and idolatry, from arrogance and blaspheming, from contempt of your Word, from disobedience and exasperation so that the sun will not set today on our anger. Amen.

HUMBLE YOURSELVES IN THE SIGHT OF THE
LORD, AND HE SHALL LIFT YOU UP.

James 4:10

LORD, AWAKEN IN US A HUNGER AND thirst for you and your righteousness. Teach us to act according to your will, for you are our God. May your good Spirit lead us along the straight path. We commend ourselves to you. Let all of our works be blessed and bring honor to your name and be useful to our neighbors. Make us into tools of your mercy, and let us joyfully go forth and practice our calling. Amen.

THOU WILT SHEW ME THE PATH OF LIFE: IN THY
PRESENCE IS FULNESS OF JOY; AT THY RIGHT HAND
THERE ARE PLEASURES FOR EVERMORE.

Psalm 16:11

Prayers
for Divine Guidance

HOLY FATHER, ALWAYS BE OUR PATH and guide, our protection and shield, our consolation and strength. Set our feet, minds, and hearts onto your path of divine peace. Make your holy and divine Word, which you allow us to hear, vibrant and active in our hearts so we might please and serve you until the end of our lives. Amen.

AND THE PEACE OF GOD, WHICH PASSETH ALL UNDERSTANDING, SHALL KEEP YOUR HEARTS AND MINDS THROUGH CHRIST JESUS.

Philippians 4:7

O LORD, ALMIGHTY GOD AND HEAVENLY Father, we ask you: Give us the honor of faith, love, loyalty, and truth. Through knowledge of your holy Word and Holy Spirit, always be our path and guide, protection and shelter. Set our souls on the way of your divine peace, that we may serve you as your dear children until our end. And as your children, let us not be tempted beyond our ability, but rather make a way for us through temptation and tribulation, that though suffering, we may endure it. We ask this, holy Father, in the name of your dear Son, our Lord and Savior Jesus Christ. Amen.

BLESSED IS THE MAN THAT ENDURETH
TEMPTATION: FOR WHEN HE IS TRIED, HE SHALL
RECEIVE THE CROWN OF LIFE, WHICH THE LORD
HATH PROMISED TO THEM THAT LOVE HIM.

James 1:12

W E ASK YOU WITH OUR WHOLE HEARTS, O holy, loving, triune God in heaven, to build us up and establish us according to your holy will. Transform us and draw us mercifully to you. Aid us, that we may follow your commandments and serve you cheerfully and willingly.

Be our gracious bridge and way. Ever set our hearts and minds on the path of your holy and divine peace so that we may willingly cling to you and serve you as your dear children. Amen.

I WILL SAY OF THE LORD,
HE IS MY REFUGE AND MY FORTRESS:
MY GOD; IN HIM WILL I TRUST.

Psalm 91:2

CREATE A PATH IN THE DARKNESS WITH your holy Word, O heavenly Father, and lead us in your holy name. May we not be scattered and forsaken, like sheep without a shepherd. You see that the harvest is bountiful and the workers few, so we ask you, O Lord of the harvest, wake up the workers, faithful shepherds and teachers, people of your holy heart who have found grace before your eyes. People who will preach your holy Word without any pride, but instead through the mercy and strength of your Holy Spirit. Amen.

AND THE SERVANT OF THE LORD MUST NOT STRIVE; BUT BE GENTLE UNTO ALL MEN, APT TO TEACH, PATIENT, IN MEEKNESS INSTRUCTING THOSE THAT OPPOSE THEMSELVES.

2 Timothy 2:24–25

W E ASK YOU, HOLY LORD, TO FAITHFULLY
bless our comings and goings, and to
protect our mouths, hearts, and minds. Set our hearts
on the path of your holy and divine peace.

We ask you, holy Father, to bind us with the bond
of peace and your pure, divine love so that we may
wholeheartedly live and walk according to your sacred
Word and will, now until the end of our lives.

We ask you this, holy Father, in the name of your
beloved Son, Jesus Christ our Lord. Amen.

WALK WORTHY OF THE VOCATION WHEREWITH
YE ARE CALLED, WITH ALL LOWLINESS AND
MEEKNESS, WITH LONGSUFFERING, FORBEARING
ONE ANOTHER IN LOVE; ENDEAVOURING TO KEEP
THE UNITY OF THE SPIRIT IN THE BOND OF PEACE.

Ephesians 4:1–3

GRANT ME FOOD AND CLOTHING, O LORD, and lead me down the path I should follow. Bless my endeavors so that everything may be done for your glory, the common good, and my welfare and that of my family. Preserve and defend my family and everything that you have given me. May we dwell together in health and in joy.

I especially ask you to protect me, my God, from all trickery and malice of the devil and his minions. Protect and strengthen me in true belief and in repentance, patience, and hope. Let me make a safe pilgrimage through this difficult life with a good conscience, until I depart and joyfully enter into the heavenly country. I commend my comings and goings to you, O Lord, from now until eternity, through Jesus Christ. Amen.

THE LORD SHALL PRESERVE THY GOING OUT AND
THY COMING IN FROM THIS TIME FORTH, AND
EVEN FOR EVERMORE.

Psalm 121:8

STRENGTHEN ME, LORD, WITH YOUR SPIRIT and your might, and give me a strong, firm faith, so I might say to you: My confidence, my God in whom I hope, save me. Let your wisdom be my shield.

O Lord, help me, for I desire you. Protect me, for I acknowledge your name. O Lord, I call on you, so hear me. Be with me in trouble, rescue me with your almighty hand, and show me eternal salvation in Jesus Christ, our dear Savior. Amen.

AND THEY THAT KNOW THY NAME WILL PUT
THEIR TRUST IN THEE: FOR THOU, LORD, HAST
NOT FORSAKEN THEM THAT SEEK THEE.

Psalm 9:10

Prayers
of Gratitude

WE HUMBLY AND WHOLEHEARTEDLY thank you, O loving Lord God, and give you all praise, honor, and glory for your great kindnesses and fatherly faithfulness, and for your tremendous gifts and mercies that you show us now and forever. We also give you heartfelt thanks, gracious, holy Father, for all that you have created: heaven and earth, the sea and everything in it. You keep faith forever, and you bring justice to those who have suffered much injustice. You have saved all those who cleave to you, those who have believed in you, trusted in you, faithfully served you, and forever remained in awe of you. Amen.

BECAUSE HE HATH SET HIS LOVE UPON ME,
THEREFORE WILL I DELIVER HIM: I WILL SET HIM
ON HIGH, BECAUSE HE HATH KNOWN MY NAME.

Psalm 91:14

FAITHFUL SAVIOR, O LOVING LORD:
We humbly and sincerely thank you for suffering and dying, and for becoming our righteousness. We thank you for the unspeakable pain and bloodshed, even death, that you suffered freely and patiently so that you might save us and release us from eternal shame and agony. Therefore, O patient, sacrificial Lamb, may you be highly praised for all eternity. Amen.

AND BEING FOUND IN FASHION AS A MAN, HE HUMBLED HIMSELF, AND BECAME OBEDIENT UNTO DEATH, EVEN THE DEATH OF THE CROSS.

Philippians 2:8

DEAR HOLY FATHER, WE GIVE YOU GREAT praise, honor, and glory, and deep gratitude for your innumerable and unspeakably glorious kindnesses and favors, indeed for all your spiritual and physical blessings, mercies, and good deeds. We offer deep and humble thanks for your great grace and rich mercy, and we especially thank you again for your eternal salvation, which you gave us through our Lord, Jesus Christ. Amen.

AND BEING MADE PERFECT, HE BECAME THE
AUTHOR OF ETERNAL SALVATION UNTO ALL THEM
THAT OBEY HIM.

Hebrews 5:9

WE THANK YOU FOR ALL THE OPPORTU-
nities we have had in which to serve you,
call on you, and pray to you, holy God and Father. Help
us daily to revere and honor you. O holy, loving Father,
Son, and Holy Spirit, may all praise, honor, glory, and
thanks be offered to you, from now to eternity. Amen.

WHEREFORE WE RECEIVING A KINGDOM WHICH
CANNOT BE MOVED, LET US HAVE GRACE,
WHEREBY WE MAY SERVE GOD ACCEPTABLY WITH
REVERENCE AND GODLY FEAR.

Hebrews 12:28

WE GIVE YOU PRAISE AND THANKS, O heavenly Father, for the unspeakably great mercy and unfathomably great love you have shown us through Jesus Christ, our Lord and Savior. You have purchased and redeemed us, Lord Jesus Christ, through your holy and costly atonement on the cross, where you let your body be broken and your blood be spilled. Thus you became a pure sacrifice, holy and complete, for us sinners, who could not have been redeemed by any sacrifice except your bitter suffering and death—something you in your great love so willingly endured for us. Amen.

BUT GOD, WHO IS RICH IN MERCY,
FOR HIS GREAT LOVE WHEREWITH HE LOVED
US, EVEN WHEN WE WERE DEAD IN SINS, HATH
QUICKENED US TOGETHER WITH CHRIST
(BY GRACE YE ARE SAVED).

Ephesians 2:4–5

THE EYES OF ALL BELIEVERS ARE ON YOU, Lord God and heavenly Father, since you are the Provider for all. Open your gentle hand and pour out your gracious blessings over those who hope in you and open their eyes to you. Give us, Lord, spiritual eyes trustingly directed toward you. May we graciously enjoy the blessing and benediction of your divine grace, and may we take in moderation that which you have given to us and use it to honor you and fulfill our needs. Above all else, nourish our souls unceasingly with the bread of your holy Word, through your dear Son, our Lord Jesus Christ. Amen.

THE LORD IS MY PORTION, SAITH MY SOUL; THEREFORE WILL I HOPE IN HIM. THE LORD IS GOOD UNTO THEM THAT WAIT FOR HIM, TO THE SOUL THAT SEEKETH HIM.

Lamentations 3:24–25

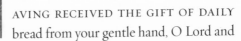

AVING RECEIVED THE GIFT OF DAILY bread from your gentle hand, O Lord and heavenly Father, and been satisfied with it—this gift which you give to us in such abundance, just as you do all your other gifts—we ask you through Christ, your Son, to make the power of the Holy Spirit complete in us. We desire to love you with our whole hearts and bless you with our mouths so that we who receive your gifts do not become proud and arrogant, nor forget your love and sacred commandments. We desire to love you with our whole hearts, not just with our mouths and lips but with our works and deeds and all that is in us. We thank you; we honor, praise, and bless you as our Creator and Sustainer, not just in this life but also in the life everlasting. Amen.

THOU SHALT LOVE THE LORD THY GOD WITH ALL
THY HEART, AND WITH ALL THY SOUL, AND WITH
ALL THY STRENGTH, AND WITH ALL THY MIND;
AND THY NEIGHBOUR AS THYSELF.

Luke 10:27

Prayers
of Repentance

ALMIGHTY GOD AND HEAVENLY FATHER, through abuse of your blessings, transgressions against your divine commandments, and failure to meet our obligations, we have passed neither this night nor the whole course of our life in a devout manner. We have sinned against you in a multitude of ways, in word, deed, and thought, asleep and awake; we confess with sorrow that it is so. But you, O heavenly Father, will forgive and wipe away our sins through your grace and through the shed blood of your dear Son, Jesus Christ. Amen.

IT IS OF THE LORD'S MERCIES THAT WE ARE NOT
CONSUMED, BECAUSE HIS COMPASSIONS FAIL NOT.
THEY ARE NEW EVERY MORNING:
GREAT IS THY FAITHFULNESS.

Lamentations 3:22–23

LORD, ALMIGHTY GOD AND HEAVENLY Father, you who know and recognize everyone's heart and failings, I ask you to help and comfort me during my great distress. Forgive me my sins and misdeeds, which I have committed against you in word or deed, action or omission, knowingly or unknowingly.

Let me acknowledge your holy Word, O Lord my God. From the bottom of my heart, I ask you to forgive me my great sins and misdeeds and do not count them against me.

Do not bring your poor servant to judgment, holy Father in heaven, but have mercy on me. As a compassionate father has mercy on his children, so also have mercy on this poor sinner. Amen.

LIKE AS A FATHER PITIETH HIS CHILDREN, SO THE
LORD PITIETH THEM THAT FEAR HIM.

Psalm 103:13

W E ASK YOU, GRACIOUS, HOLY FATHER, to have mercy on us now and for all of our lives, but especially in these last, dangerous times. Forgive us all of our sins and misdeeds, the secret and the public, the known and the unknown. Pardon and forgive us everything that we have done against you—whether it was done knowingly or unknowingly, with words or with deeds, secretly or openly—both what is contrary to our better judgment and conscience, and what is contrary to your law and your holy Scripture. We ask you humbly and wholeheartedly to be gracious and merciful, O holy Father, for Jesus Christ's sake. Amen.

WITHHOLD NOT THOU THY TENDER MERCIES
FROM ME, O LORD: LET THY LOVINGKINDNESS
AND THY TRUTH CONTINUALLY PRESERVE ME.

Psalm 40:11

HOLY FATHER, WE PRAY FOR ALL PEOPLE who call upon your holy name with penitent hearts, who know and recognize their inner failings and afflictions, and who desire your mercy and the intercession of the faithful. Be gracious to us, Lord in heaven, and deal justly with us according to your wisdom, for you know each heart, mind, thought, and motive. All secrets are revealed in the light of your presence. Give us now, O Lord, wisdom from above, that we may deeply revere you in all things. Amen.

WISDOM IS THE PRINCIPAL THING;
THEREFORE GET WISDOM: AND WITH ALL
THY GETTING GET UNDERSTANDING.

Proverbs 4:7

LORD, I HAVE BEEN DISOBEDIENT. I confess this with a humble heart and come to you like a child to his father and say: I am heartily afraid because of my great sin. I have sinned, O Father, and done evil before you. Oh, have mercy on me, I beg you from the bottom of my heart, and save me from my temptation. O Father, comfort me again with your fatherly aid. I call on you from my heart like David, dear God and Father! Create in me a clean heart, O God, and give me a right spirit, that I may from this day forward serve you humbly and wholeheartedly in love and trust, in safety, and with childlike hope. Amen.

CREATE IN ME A CLEAN HEART, O GOD; AND
RENEW A RIGHT SPIRIT WITHIN ME.

Psalm 51:10

I ACKNOWLEDGE THAT I HAVE PROVOKED your righteous anger with my innumerable sins, O merciful, holy God; you are just and your judgment is righteous. Oh, how sorry I am that I have distressed you so often and so much, my dearest Father, and been so unthankful for your great kindnesses. Do not be angry, O Lord, and do not consider the sins of my youth or my transgressions, but remember me according to your mercy, for the sake of your lovingkindness.

This is your just punishment, O Lord, which I properly suffer because I sinned against you. But I turn my eyes of faith to your throne of grace, my Lord Jesus Christ, and bend the knees of my heart before you, asking for mercy and forgiveness. Amen.

REMEMBER NOT THE SINS OF MY YOUTH,
NOR MY TRANSGRESSIONS:
ACCORDING TO THY MERCY REMEMBER THOU ME
FOR THY GOODNESS' SAKE, O LORD.

Psalm 25:7

REMEMBER, LORD, YOUR MERCY AND your kindness, which you have shown since the dawn of time. Do not remember the sins of our youth, nor our wrongdoing, but remember us according to your mercy, for the sake of your goodness.

Give us true repentance, heartfelt remorse, and grief over our sins, O Lord Jesus—a godly sorrow, one that prepares our hearts to receive your comfort and forgiveness. Give us the spirit of love, gentleness, humility, devotion, reverence, mercy, and prayer so that we and all the saints may possess your kingdom with love and eternal life. Amen.

BUT THE FRUIT OF THE SPIRIT IS
LOVE, JOY, PEACE, LONGSUFFERING,
GENTLENESS, GOODNESS, FAITH.

Galatians 5:22

Prayers
for Comfort

HOLY FATHER IN HEAVEN, WE PRAY FOR all the widows and orphans, for the elderly and infirm, for those who have declined mentally, for all the sick, the abandoned, the desolate, the hungry, and the needy. We pray also for those with troubled minds and those despairing and despondent. O Lord, they are all well known to you. Console them with your divine comfort. Amen.

DEFEND THE POOR AND FATHERLESS: DO JUSTICE
TO THE AFFLICTED AND NEEDY.

Psalm 82:3

DEAR FATHER, AS DAVID SAYS: THE LITTLE that a righteous man has is better than the riches of the godless. I was young and I became old, yet I have never seen the righteous forsaken, nor their children begging for bread. This promise comforts and satisfies me, for it is better to have little with righteousness than to have much with unrighteousness. For we came into this world with nothing, and we will leave it with nothing.

Therefore, I ask you to give me a heart that concerns itself more with eternal, spiritual wealth than worldly goods; you will make sure I receive my humble portion. Let me follow the beautiful teaching of the wise house preacher who said: Trust in God and remain in your station, because it is easy for the Lord to make a poor man rich. Amen.

BUT GODLINESS WITH CONTENTMENT IS GREAT GAIN. FOR WE BROUGHT NOTHING INTO THIS WORLD, AND IT IS CERTAIN WE CAN CARRY NOTHING OUT. AND HAVING FOOD AND RAIMENT LET US BE THEREWITH CONTENT.

1 Timothy 6:6–8

W E CALL ON YOU TODAY TO COME TO US, Holy Spirit. Bring a spark of your divine brightness to our dark, gloomy hearts so that we may see the eternal light and rightly perceive Jesus Christ.

Come, Father of miserable orphans! Come, gentle Giver of all good gifts! Come, Purifier of all impure hearts! Come and do your work in us; sanctify us and stir in us what you, Christ, received from the Father and passed on to us poor people so we might desire your heart. Comfort and strengthen us, and stand by us in our troubles and temptations, both those stemming from the inborn sins of our flesh as well as those of the world and the devil.

Cleanse our minds of all impurity and evil that we may please God in everything, so we might walk with discipline and righteousness in this world and be known as children of God. Amen.

LET THE WORDS OF MY MOUTH,
AND THE MEDITATION OF MY HEART, BE
ACCEPTABLE IN THY SIGHT, O LORD, MY
STRENGTH, AND MY REDEEMER.

Psalm 19:14

DEAREST COMFORTER OF DESOLATE hearts and worthy guest of believing souls, sweet refreshment and strength in our weakness, do not abandon us, but with God the Father and the Son create an eternal dwelling in us. Sharpen our dullness, cleanse our impurity, heal our infirmities, make straight the lame and the crooked, and renew those who have grown cold. Lead back to the right path those who have strayed or are lost. Amen.

BY MERCY AND TRUTH INIQUITY IS
PURGED: AND BY THE FEAR OF THE
LORD MEN DEPART FROM EVIL.

Proverbs 16:6

HOLY SPIRIT, CULTIVATE IN US YOUR sevenfold gifts: the gift of divine wisdom; a right new understanding of God's Word and will; the gift of counsel to the praise of His glory; the gift of spiritual strength and power; the true knowledge of God and Christ; the gift of the fear of the Lord; and godliness. Share these gracious gifts with your poor, forsaken people because of your unspeakable love and goodness, and for the sake of Him who redeemed us with His precious blood. Amen.

THAT YE MIGHT WALK WORTHY OF THE LORD
UNTO ALL PLEASING, BEING FRUITFUL IN
EVERY GOOD WORK, AND INCREASING IN THE
KNOWLEDGE OF GOD; STRENGTHENED WITH ALL
MIGHT, ACCORDING TO HIS GLORIOUS POWER,
UNTO ALL PATIENCE AND LONGSUFFERING
WITH JOYFULNESS.

Colossians 1:10–11

OLY SPIRIT, CAPTURE OUR HEARTS WITH your loving strength. Fill them with heavenly comfort and joy so that we may always rest assured in God and face our concerns with joy and contentment, and so as children of God overcome this evil world. Praise be to you forever and ever, Holy Spirit, along with God the Father and the Son! Amen.

BLESSED BE GOD, EVEN THE FATHER OF OUR LORD JESUS CHRIST, THE FATHER OF MERCIES, AND THE GOD OF ALL COMFORT; WHO COMFORTETH US IN ALL OUR TRIBULATION, THAT WE MAY BE ABLE TO COMFORT THEM WHICH ARE IN ANY TROUBLE, BY THE COMFORT WHEREWITH WE OURSELVES ARE COMFORTED OF GOD.

2 Corinthians 1:3–4

I COME TO YOU, DEAR GOD, IN MY weakness and misery, and ask sincerely that you listen, for you say in your Word that you will listen to the miserable. O dear Father, hear me for the sake of Jesus Christ, for I am deeply afraid. O Lord, hear me in my great dread, for you have saved all who have called on you with their whole hearts. I humbly call on you in Jesus' name: Come to this poor wretch's aid, else I will die. The waves of grief beat on my boat, O God, and it seems ready to sink. Therefore I call on you from the very depths of my soul: O God, come help me, just as you helped Jairus's daughter, before I sink in my anguish! Amen.

YE SHALL BE SORROWFUL, BUT YOUR SORROW
SHALL BE TURNED INTO JOY.

John 16:20

Prayers
of *Praise*

WE SHOULD PRAISE AND BLESS YOU ABOVE all else, O holy Father in heaven, for you are our God and Creator. You molded and made us in your image, and you have blessed us much more than any other creature.

And for this we acknowledge, O holy Father, that we, more than any other creature, owe you praise, thanksgiving, and blessing. Therefore we fall to our knees before you. Amen.

THIS PEOPLE HAVE I FORMED FOR MYSELF; THEY SHALL SHEW FORTH MY PRAISE.

Isaiah 43:21

WE GIVE YOU PRAISE AND THANKS, glory and honor, and eternal blessing, O holy Father in heaven, that you have had mercy on us. You have given us food and drink, clothing and shelter, sanctuary and sustenance for body and soul. All good things come from you alone, O Lord. Give them to us to use according to your holy will.

We ask you all this, O holy Father, in the name of your dear Son, Jesus Christ, along with the strength and assistance of the Holy Spirit. May you be highly praised, glorified, and blessed now and forever. Amen, amen.

PRAISE YE THE LORD. SING UNTO THE LORD A NEW SONG, AND HIS PRAISE IN THE CONGREGATION OF SAINTS.

Psalm 149:1

WE GIVE YOU PRAISE AND THANKS, HOLY Father, for you have created everything: heaven and earth, the sea and everything that is upon and within it. You are forever faithful; you give justice to those suffering injustice. You have saved all who have believed and trusted in you since the dawn of time, all who fear you. We ask you to give us a steadfast, living faith, a firm trust, a holy hope and a perfect love so that we may serve you wholeheartedly, with all our life and strength until our very end. Amen.

THOU WILT KEEP HIM IN PERFECT PEACE,
WHOSE MIND IS STAYED ON THEE: BECAUSE HE
TRUSTETH IN THEE.

Isaiah 26:3

ALMIGHTY FATHER IN YOUR ETERNAL kingdom, we give you praise and thanks for your unspeakably great grace and mercy, and for eternal salvation through your beloved Son, our dear Lord and Savior Jesus Christ. O Lord Christ, you suffered and endured bitter agony and death, the shedding of your innocent blood, to redeem us from eternal humiliation and pain. Father, Son, and Holy Spirit, may you above all things be highly praised, honored, and blessed from now until eternity. Amen.

AND THE WORD WAS MADE FLESH,
AND DWELT AMONG US,
(AND WE BEHELD HIS GLORY, THE GLORY AS OF
THE ONLY BEGOTTEN OF THE FATHER,)
FULL OF GRACE AND TRUTH.

John 1:14

HOLY FATHER, MAY WE SHINE AS A LIGHT in the world so that when others see the chaste path we follow in Christ, they may be won over and edified through our example, even without instruction. May this serve to praise and honor your holy name, and to bring comfort and salvation and eternal life through Jesus Christ our Lord.

O Lord, almighty God and heavenly Father! For the love and faithfulness that you demonstrate to us at all hours of every day, we faithfully praise and thank you. May you be praised forever and ever, O Lord, now and always. Amen.

BUT SANCTIFY THE LORD GOD IN YOUR HEARTS: AND BE READY ALWAYS TO GIVE AN ANSWER TO EVERY MAN THAT ASKETH YOU A REASON OF THE HOPE THAT IS IN YOU WITH MEEKNESS AND FEAR.

1 Peter 3:15

O GRACIOUS, KIND, LOVING LORD JESUS Christ! Gentle, humble, patient Lord! You left us a beautiful, virtuous example of a holy life so that we might follow in your footsteps. You are an immaculate mirror of all virtues, a perfect example of holiness, an irreproachable measure of piety, and a sure standard of righteousness. How different my sinful life is compared to your just life! Amen.

HE RESTORETH MY SOUL: HE LEADETH
ME IN THE PATHS OF RIGHTEOUSNESS
FOR HIS NAME'S SAKE.

Psalm 23:3

M Y ONLY CONFIDENCE, MY LOVE AND my hope, my honor, my adornment! Your life has been nothing other than love, meekness, and humility. Let your precious life be in me; let your virtuous life be my life. Let me be one spirit, body, and soul with you so that I may live in you and you in me; rather than I myself, may you live in me. Let me acknowledge you and love you so that I may walk as you have walked. As you are my light, so shine in me; as you are my life, so live in me; as you are my faith, so adorn me; as you are my joy, so be pleased with me; as I am your dwelling, so dwell in me. Let me be your instrument so that my body, soul, and mind are holy. Amen.

AND BE NOT CONFORMED TO THIS WORLD: BUT
BE YE TRANSFORMED BY THE RENEWING OF YOUR
MIND, THAT YE MAY PROVE WHAT IS THAT GOOD,
AND ACCEPTABLE, AND PERFECT, WILL OF GOD.

Romans 12:2

WHEN YOU, O GOD, EMERGE IN SPLENDOR from your ivory palace, your garments are noble myrrh, aloe, and cassia. You are the King of Glory, strong and powerful, mighty in battle. Fling wide the door and unbar the gate so that the King of Glory may enter!

Blessed is he who comes in the name of the Lord, the Lord God who enlightens us. O Lord, aid us so that we will succeed! You have removed sin, curses, and death, and you have blessed us eternally in heavenly places. Give your people power, strength, and victory over all spiritual and physical enemies. Amen.

THE LORD IS GOOD UNTO THEM THAT WAIT
FOR HIM, TO THE SOUL THAT SEEKETH HIM. IT
IS GOOD THAT A MAN SHOULD BOTH HOPE AND
QUIETLY WAIT FOR THE SALVATION OF THE LORD.

Lamentations 3:25–26

GOD, YOU CREATED ME TO PRAISE YOU; make me worthy of your love. You are the noblest, most praiseworthy, the holiest, most righteous, most beautiful, most benevolent, the kindest, and the truest. You are just in all your works and holy in all your ways. You are the most wise, and you know all your works from eternity past. You are all-powerful, and none may withstand you. Amen.

THINE, O LORD, IS THE GREATNESS, AND THE
POWER, AND THE GLORY, AND THE VICTORY,
AND THE MAJESTY: FOR ALL THAT IS IN THE
HEAVEN AND IN THE EARTH IS THINE; THINE IS THE
KINGDOM, O LORD, AND THOU ART EXALTED AS
HEAD ABOVE ALL.

1 Chronicles 29:11

O ETERNAL LIGHT, ETERNAL SALVATION, eternal love, eternal sweetness, let me see you, let me feel you, let me taste you. O eternal delight, eternal consolation, eternal happiness, let me dwell in you; everything I lack in my misery I find in you. You are all abundance, and apart from you is nothing but poverty, woe, and misery. Life without you is a bitter death. Your kindness is better than life itself. Amen.

> BECAUSE THY LOVINGKINDNESS IS BETTER THAN
> LIFE, MY LIPS SHALL PRAISE THEE. THUS WILL
> I BLESS THEE WHILE I LIVE: I WILL LIFT UP MY
> HANDS IN THY NAME.
>
> Psalm 63:3–4

O PRICELESS TREASURE, ETERNAL GOOD, sweet life, when will I be completely one with you, so that I may fully see you? Holy, immortal, righteous, all-wise God, eternal King, may you receive praise, honor, and glory for all eternity. Amen.

FOR NOW WE SEE THROUGH A GLASS, DARKLY; BUT THEN FACE TO FACE: NOW I KNOW IN PART; BUT THEN SHALL I KNOW EVEN AS ALSO I AM KNOWN.

1 Corinthians 13:12

Prayers
for Strength

ALMIGHTY GOD AND HEAVENLY FATHER, I ask you with all my heart, give me true faith, hope, and love, through which I may become holy and blessed. I ask you, holy Father, make me strong in my weakness and healthy in my sickness, both in soul and body. So clothe me, holy Father, in the armor of your divine power that I may triumph against the cunning attack of the evil enemy, who fights against your truth. Give me the shield of genuine faith so that I might have victory against those who would prevent me from living out your love and justice. Amen.

FINALLY, MY BRETHREN, BE STRONG IN THE LORD,
AND IN THE POWER OF HIS MIGHT. PUT ON THE
WHOLE ARMOUR OF GOD, THAT YE MAY BE ABLE
TO STAND AGAINST THE WILES OF THE DEVIL.

Ephesians 6:10–11

W<small>E ASK YOU</small>, L<small>ORD</small> J<small>ESUS</small> C<small>HRIST</small>, <small>TO</small> deliver us from all our troubles, and to help us become children of peace through your encouraging eternal Gospel truth. Lift us with your grace and power, strengthen the weak, and assist the strong to follow your Word. Let us not be concerned with anything but your glory and our souls' salvation. Help us forget all our hearts' temporal and earthly concerns and only strive earnestly for that which is eternal and of you. Grant us this for your sake, Jesus Christ, you who live and reign with God your Father and the Holy Spirit, true God now and forever! Amen.

<small>BLESSED ARE THE PEACEMAKERS: FOR THEY</small>
<small>SHALL BE CALLED THE CHILDREN OF GOD.</small>

Matthew 5:9

O LORD GOD, ALMIGHTY, HEAVENLY, merciful Father, give us poor, needy, miserable people the spirit of wisdom and the revelation of your knowledge. Enlighten the eyes of our understanding, and strengthen and grow our faith in Jesus Christ. Give us an unquestioning hope in your mercy, despite the stupidity of our sinful consciences. Give us a sound, righteous love for you and all people, for your sake. We ask you that you strengthen our poor, weak consciences and that you give us the vibrant, real power of your mighty Word through the Holy Spirit. Amen.

LET US THEREFORE COME BOLDLY UNTO THE
THRONE OF GRACE, THAT WE MAY OBTAIN MERCY,
AND FIND GRACE TO HELP IN TIME OF NEED.

Hebrews 4:16

O LORD, WE RECOGNIZE THE HOPE OF our calling, the wealth of the glorious inheritance of your saints, and the overwhelming greatness of your strength in those who believe in you. This came about by your mighty power, which you worked in Christ when you raised Him from the dead and set Him at your right hand in heaven, above all principalities, forces, powers, rulers, and everything that may be so named not only in this world but also in the next. Since we are yours and are here to praise your glory, heavenly Father, give us all of this in our hearts, spirits, and minds through the Holy Spirit and Jesus Christ, your Son and our Lord, through whom you have promised to give us all things, according to your holy, perfect will. Amen.

GIVING THANKS UNTO THE FATHER, WHICH
HATH MADE US MEET TO BE PARTAKERS OF THE
INHERITANCE OF THE SAINTS IN LIGHT: WHO HATH
DELIVERED US FROM THE POWER OF DARKNESS,
AND HATH TRANSLATED US INTO THE KINGDOM
OF HIS DEAR SON.

Colossians 1:12–13

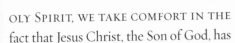

HOLY SPIRIT, WE TAKE COMFORT IN THE fact that Jesus Christ, the Son of God, has had mercy on us. We give Him thanks and praise for this, with the sincere hope that He will never abandon us. Without ceasing, He represents us to His heavenly Father; indeed, He does so for all who have surrendered themselves to Him.

Inasmuch as you, Holy Spirit, are the Spirit of the Lord Jesus Christ, let us also enjoy such devotion, love, and kindness. Pour your mighty strength into us, and give those who are weak in faith, yet who submit themselves to you in word and truth, a new, reborn heart. Amen.

THEREFORE IF ANY MAN BE IN CHRIST, HE IS A
NEW CREATURE: OLD THINGS ARE PASSED AWAY;
BEHOLD, ALL THINGS ARE BECOME NEW.

2 Corinthians 5:17

O LORD, LIKE YOUR SERVANT DAVID, THE fear in my heart is great. He, too, called on you in great need, when his heart quaked and never expected to be happy again. Look at me, dear Father, and see that it is the same with me. I sometimes think that there is no hope left to summon. Oh, how often do I think of these words: Misery has surrounded me, wretchedness has done me in. I am dismayed that it is so, dear Father, but I know that you understand more than I can tell you, and therefore I beg you even more, have pity on me. Comfort me, O Lord! Amen.

PEACE I LEAVE WITH YOU, MY PEACE I GIVE
UNTO YOU: NOT AS THE WORLD GIVETH, GIVE I
UNTO YOU. LET NOT YOUR HEART BE TROUBLED,
NEITHER LET IT BE AFRAID.

John 14:27

O LORD, HELP ME! WEAK AND ANXIOUS AS I am, like the impure woman,[1] if I could touch the hem of your robe, I would be made well. Strengthen me in my weakness, just as you strengthened your servant[2] who was just as fearful, saying: Let me and my grace be enough for you. Amen.

BUT THEY THAT WAIT UPON THE LORD SHALL
RENEW THEIR STRENGTH; THEY SHALL MOUNT UP
WITH WINGS AS EAGLES; THEY SHALL RUN,
AND NOT BE WEARY; AND THEY SHALL WALK,
AND NOT FAINT.

Isaiah 40:31

1. See Mark 5:28–29.
2. This probably refers to Paul, to whom the Lord said, "My grace is sufficient for thee" (2 Corinthians 12:9).

OH, DEAR FATHER! I CONFESS THAT I AM so overwhelmed that I can say with David: I am withered like grass. There is nothing left in me that can refresh me; only you can do that. Yes, I must say that I fade away like an evening shadow, but you can revive me if you choose to, for your miracles are many. I cry to you with Jonah, O Lord, from the bottom of my despairing heart. I call to you with that blind man: Have mercy on me, O Jesus, Son of David! You can help me if you choose to. Amen.

THE LORD THY GOD IN THE MIDST OF THEE IS MIGHTY; HE WILL SAVE, HE WILL REJOICE OVER THEE WITH JOY; HE WILL REST IN HIS LOVE, HE WILL JOY OVER THEE WITH SINGING.

Zephaniah 3:17

G IVE US THE STRENGTH, LORD JESUS, TO strive for the richness of your glory, to become strong in our inner being through your Spirit. May you live in our hearts through faith, and be rooted and planted through love. May we come to know how high and how deep your love is. May we have love for our fellow Christians and be filled with all of God's abundance, which is better than all knowledge.

Therefore, keep us in faith, secure us in love, strengthen us in hope. Come and dwell in us, O Holy Trinity. Fill us here on earth with your mercy and there with your eternal glory. Hear our prayer: Give us your Holy Spirit, who will enlighten us with your divine Word to make us holy, and to teach, strengthen, ground, and preserve us unto eternal life. Amen.

THAT HE WOULD GRANT YOU, ACCORDING TO
THE RICHES OF HIS GLORY, TO BE STRENGTHENED
WITH MIGHT BY HIS SPIRIT IN THE INNER MAN . . .
AND TO KNOW THE LOVE OF CHRIST, WHICH
PASSETH KNOWLEDGE, THAT YE MIGHT BE FILLED
WITH ALL THE FULNESS OF GOD.

Ephesians 3:16, 19

Prayers
for Purity of Heart

OLY FATHER, REMOVE ALL THE SIN THAT binds and oppresses us: anger, disgust, envy, hatred, lust, pride, and greed, the root of all evil. And cleanse our evil hearts of all unrighteousness. Create in us a clean heart, O Lord, and renew in us a sincere and willing spirit. Teach us your ways, and give us grace so that we may walk within them until the end of our days. Amen.

THE LORD IS NIGH UNTO THEM THAT ARE OF A
BROKEN HEART; AND SAVETH SUCH AS BE OF A
CONTRITE SPIRIT.

Psalm 34:18

O HOLY FATHER IN HEAVEN: PROTECT ME from sin as a merciful father would; release me and free me from it. Cleanse me with living water so that I may now and forever wholeheartedly say: Our Father, which art in heaven, hallowed be thy name. Thy kingdom come, thy will be done in earth, as it is in heaven. Give us this day our daily bread. And forgive us our debts, as we forgive our debtors. And lead us not into temptation, but deliver us from evil: For thine is the kingdom, and the power, and the glory, forever. Amen.

AFTER THIS MANNER THEREFORE PRAY YE: OUR FATHER WHICH ART IN HEAVEN. . . .

Matthew 6:9

O NOBLE, HOLY, PURE, UNBLEMISHED LORD Jesus Christ, lover of purity, crown of all honor and virtue, I deplore and confess the innate impurity of my heart. I have often defiled my body and soul through impure thoughts, words, and deeds. Oh, you whose heart is kind and pure, forgive me my great sin and turn aside the severe punishment by which you admonish the unrighteous.

For as the pure of heart, who see God, are blessed, so the unrighteous, who do not see God, are surely wretched. Therefore, create in me, O God, a clean heart, and do not cast me from your holy presence because of my impurity. Amen.

IF WE CONFESS OUR SINS, HE IS FAITHFUL AND
JUST TO FORGIVE US OUR SINS, AND TO CLEANSE
US FROM ALL UNRIGHTEOUSNESS.

1 John 1:9

O GOD, BECAUSE I ACKNOWLEDGE THAT I can only live with discipline, you give me that discipline; such knowledge is a great mercy. Thus I ask you most humbly: Cleanse my heart and make it holy through repentance and faith, through the Holy Spirit and through rebirth. Strengthen me, so I do not let any impure spirit control or possess me. Amen.

DRAW NIGH TO GOD,
AND HE WILL DRAW NIGH TO YOU.

James 4:8

SURROUND MY HEART WITH YOUR PURE love, chaste and noble Bridegroom of my soul. Unite and marry my soul to your pure heart. Fill my heart with holy and pure thoughts so that I may be and always remain an untainted part of your body. Let me not become an impure vessel of dishonor but rather a vessel of mercy and honor. In this way I will not waste or lose the gifts that you have placed within me. Amen.

WHO GAVE HIMSELF FOR US, THAT HE MIGHT
REDEEM US FROM ALL INIQUITY,
AND PURIFY UNTO HIMSELF A PECULIAR PEOPLE,
ZEALOUS OF GOOD WORKS.

Titus 2:14

O NOBLE, CHASTE, CELESTIAL BRIDEGROOM, who feasts beneath the roses of purity, feed my soul with your knowledge and pure love. Drive all evil thoughts from me so that your Holy Spirit may live in me and the holy angels may stay with me forevermore. Amen.

FINALLY, BRETHREN, WHATSOEVER THINGS ARE TRUE, WHATSOEVER THINGS ARE HONEST, WHATSOEVER THINGS ARE JUST, WHATSOEVER THINGS ARE PURE, WHATSOEVER THINGS ARE LOVELY, WHATSOEVER THINGS ARE OF GOOD REPORT; IF THERE BE ANY VIRTUE, AND IF THERE BE ANY PRAISE, THINK ON THESE THINGS.

Philippians 4:8

COME INTO MY HEART, KING OF GRACE; come and soothe my anxious heart. Make me poor and humble, just as you were when you came into this world. Let me sorrow over my sins; let me hunger and thirst for your righteousness so that I may eternally prosper through you. Come as a righteous man to this miserable sinner and make me virtuous. Clothe me in your righteousness, since God has made you my righteousness, sanctification, and redemption. Come, King of peace, and give me a peaceable, calm conscience, and prepare me for your everlasting peace and rest. Make me meek, merciful, and pure of heart. Amen.

I WILL GREATLY REJOICE IN THE LORD, MY SOUL
SHALL BE JOYFUL IN MY GOD; FOR HE HATH
CLOTHED ME WITH THE GARMENTS OF SALVATION,
HE HATH COVERED ME WITH THE ROBE OF
RIGHTEOUSNESS.

Isaiah 61:10

OME, KING OF GRACE, AND FILL ME WITH your grace in this life, just as you will fill me in heaven with your eternal glory. Reign over me in the gracious kingdom of your Holy Spirit; yes, prepare your kingdom in me, which is justice, peace, and joy in the Holy Spirit. Enlighten my heart, rule my life, and sanctify my thoughts so that they all may be reverent and pleasing to you. Surround me with your grace, that I may never be removed from it. Come to me, Holy Trinity! Make me your dwelling and your temple. Spark in me the light of your knowledge, faith, love, hope, humility, patience, prayer, perseverance, and reverence. Amen.

FOR THOU ART MY LAMP, O LORD: AND THE
LORD WILL LIGHTEN MY DARKNESS.

2 Samuel 22:29

O LORD, HEAVENLY FATHER, FROM WHOM all good and perfect gifts come; O Father of light, who causes us both to desire and to do your good pleasure; O Lord Jesus Christ, the author and perfecter of faith; O Holy Spirit, who works in all things according to your plan: We ask you to continue the good work that you began in us, until the coming of Jesus Christ. May we become richer in all kinds of knowledge and experience so we may learn what is best. May we remain pure and blameless. May we be filled with the fruits of righteousness, which were produced in us by Jesus Christ, for the glory of God. Amen.

BEING CONFIDENT OF THIS VERY THING, THAT HE WHICH HATH BEGUN A GOOD WORK IN YOU WILL PERFORM IT UNTIL THE DAY OF JESUS CHRIST.

Philippians 1:6

Prayers
for Unity

WE ASK YOU, HOLY FATHER, TO HAVE mercy on us and draw us together under your protection. Do not let dissension or separation (which do not reflect your divine will) form among us, and protect us, O Lord, from false belief and evil understanding, especially against that which would confuse or separate us from your love and righteousness. Amen.

NOW I BESEECH YOU, BRETHREN, BY THE NAME OF OUR LORD JESUS CHRIST, THAT YE ALL SPEAK THE SAME THING, AND THAT THERE BE NO DIVISIONS AMONG YOU; BUT THAT YE BE PERFECTLY JOINED TOGETHER IN THE SAME MIND AND IN THE SAME JUDGMENT.

1 Corinthians 1:10

WE ASK YOU, HOLY FATHER, TO GRACIOUSLY have mercy on all of us in the whole wide world. Bring us together under your blessing, protection, and shield, and let there be neither discord nor division among us.

Yes, graciously protect us, especially from that which would harm us or prevent our well-being and salvation, and that which would divide or confuse us, or keep us from your holy Word. Amen.

AND ALL THINGS ARE OF GOD, WHO HATH
RECONCILED US TO HIMSELF BY JESUS CHRIST,
AND HATH GIVEN TO US THE MINISTRY OF
RECONCILIATION.

2 Corinthians 5:18

YOU KNOW THE HEARTS AND SHORT-comings of all people, almighty God and heavenly Father. We ask you to give us your grace, O holy Father in heaven, as we gather together and call on the name of your dear Child, Jesus, our Savior.

Give us a real faith and genuine love, O Father, with faithfulness and truth and the power of your Holy Spirit. Do this so we might—with our whole hearts, the breath of our souls, and willing minds—honor, fear, and love you above all things, O Father, and follow your commands until the end of our life. We ask this in the name of our Lord Jesus Christ. Amen.

TILL WE ALL COME IN THE UNITY OF THE FAITH,
AND OF THE KNOWLEDGE OF THE SON OF GOD,
UNTO A PERFECT MAN, UNTO THE MEASURE OF
THE STATURE OF THE FULNESS OF CHRIST.

Ephesians 4:13

ETERNAL, MERCIFUL GOD, YOU ARE A GOD of peace, love, and unity, not of conflict or division. You rule the world justly, and you alone can establish and maintain unity. You will pass judgment on those who abandoned and rejected you, most especially in those things that concern your divine truth and the salvation of souls. O Lover of unity, you let the world divide and scatter so that it might be disgraced in its supposed wisdom and so return to you. Amen.

FOR THE WISDOM OF THIS WORLD
IS FOOLISHNESS WITH GOD.

1 Corinthians 3:19

O GOD, WE ASK AND IMPLORE YOU TO bring all that is scattered back together through the Holy Spirit, to reunite what is divided and make it whole. Grant that we may search for your eternal truth in unity, and retreat from all discord. Grant also that we may become one mind, will, conscience, nature, and understanding, which is directed toward Jesus Christ our Lord. Heavenly Father of our Lord Jesus Christ, in this unity may we honor and praise you, with one voice, through the same Lord Jesus Christ, in the Holy Spirit. Amen.

BEHOLD, HOW GOOD AND HOW PLEASANT IT IS
FOR BRETHREN TO DWELL TOGETHER IN UNITY!

Psalm 133:1

Prayers
of *Humility*

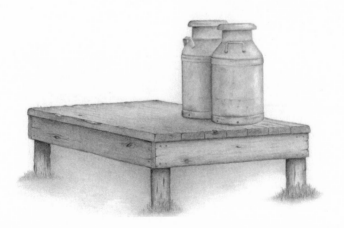

WE ASK YOU, ALMIGHTY GOD AND heavenly Father, who knows all of our shortcomings and weaknesses, and without whose help and mercy we could neither do nor be anything: Give us grace, that together we may call on you in spirit and in truth. May this, O Lord, serve to praise, honor, and glorify you, and bring all of us consolation, salvation, and eternal life. Amen.

AND BECAUSE YE ARE SONS, GOD HATH SENT
FORTH THE SPIRIT OF HIS SON INTO YOUR
HEARTS, CRYING, ABBA, FATHER.

Galatians 4:6

WE ASK YOU, HOLY FATHER, HAVE MERCY on us, as a compassionate father has mercy on his children. Send your holy angel down from above to serve as a guide, that he might go before us and fight against our foes and critics, and save us from the clutches of those who hate you. Protect us until such time that you see we are able to suffer and endure all that you have set over us, and may we not waver from your holy Word, neither to the left nor to the right. This we ask you, holy Father, in the name of Jesus Christ! Amen.

BUT THE MERCY OF THE LORD IS FROM EVERLASTING TO EVERLASTING UPON THEM THAT FEAR HIM, AND HIS RIGHTEOUSNESS UNTO CHILDREN'S CHILDREN.

Psalm 103:17

O LORD ALMIGHTY, ETERNAL, GOOD, AND gracious God, merciful heavenly Father of Christ Jesus our Lord, you are the one who best understands all our faults and our emptiness; you know that we are nothing and have nothing. Without your holy blessing, support, help, and mercy, we are incapable of doing anything.

So we ask you very humbly from our hearts, dear holy Father in heaven: Give us grace that together we might pray to you aright. Help us always; give us your holy, gracious blessing so we might pray with reverence, in spirit and in truth. May you accept our prayer and raise it up so that it may serve you and your fame, to your great glory, praise, and honor. Amen.

BUT THE HOUR COMETH, AND NOW IS, WHEN THE
TRUE WORSHIPPERS SHALL WORSHIP THE FATHER
IN SPIRIT AND IN TRUTH: FOR THE FATHER
SEEKETH SUCH TO WORSHIP HIM.

John 4:23

HOLY FATHER, WE PRAY WHOLEHEARTEDLY for all of your people, indeed for all their concerns, and for those who sincerely desire your grace and our intercession. Grant all of us your gracious, helping hand, your mercy, comfort, hope, faith, and love. Strengthen us all in genuine, true faith; in hope and patience; in true Christian love, faithfulness, and unity. O loving Father in heaven, graciously unite us with your noble, loving peace, for Christ Jesus' sake. Amen.

NOW THE GOD OF PATIENCE AND CONSOLATION
GRANT YOU TO BE LIKEMINDED ONE TOWARD
ANOTHER ACCORDING TO CHRIST JESUS:
THAT YE MAY WITH ONE MIND AND ONE MOUTH
GLORIFY GOD, EVEN THE FATHER OF OUR
LORD JESUS CHRIST.

Romans 15:5–6

**D**EAR HOLY FATHER, HAVE MERCY ON US, just as a loving father has mercy on his children.

Aid us so that we do not deviate from your holy Word, neither to the right nor to the left. Prepare for us at all times a path and a way, a place and a home, peace and an escort, that in our homes and in all our actions we may be safe from our enemies. Look mercifully upon our great weaknesses, and always bring us together in your name to listen usefully and fruitfully to your holy Word. Gather us graciously together under your mighty hand, and shelter us under your fatherly protection and shield. Keep us under your divine grace and power, which cannot be overcome. Amen.

THY WORD IS A LAMP UNTO MY FEET, AND A
LIGHT UNTO MY PATH.

Psalm 119:105

ALMIGHTY, KIND, MERCIFUL, HEAVENLY God and Father, Lord of heaven and earth: We come again to you as your children, and we ask you, holy Father, to give us your grace from on high, that we may call on you and pray to you in spirit and in truth, in faith and in the right, pure love of God, with wisdom and with awe, in humility and in submission. Amen.

AND HE SAID UNTO ME, MY GRACE IS SUFFICIENT
FOR THEE: FOR MY STRENGTH IS MADE PERFECT
IN WEAKNESS. MOST GLADLY THEREFORE WILL
I RATHER GLORY IN MY INFIRMITIES, THAT THE
POWER OF CHRIST MAY REST UPON ME.

2 Corinthians 12:9

W E ASK YOU FAITHFULLY, HOLY FATHER, TO give our hearts wisdom and understanding from on high so that we sufficiently recognize our sins and desist from them, turn from them, and repent.

We ask you, holy Father, to give us the grace to love you above all things, with our whole hearts, with the breath of our souls, and with all our strength and resources. Amen.

REJOICE IN THE LORD ALWAYS:
AND AGAIN I SAY, REJOICE.

Philippians 4:4

WE ASK YOU, HOLY FATHER, TO GIVE US grace that we may live and walk in such a way that we may always be recognized as your servants, who are waiting for their Lord. Whenever you start the wedding feast, may you find us ready and willing, Lord, every hour of every day. Amen.

BLESSED ARE THOSE SERVANTS, WHOM THE LORD
WHEN HE COMETH SHALL FIND WATCHING.

Luke 12:37

WE FAITHFULLY ASK YOU, O HOLY FATHER, to give us grace so we might raise our children in true Christian virtues; indeed, so we might set them a good example in learning, life, and behavior. May they be edified and improved through our lives and walk, and may the number of your holy chosen children be increased and fulfilled through us and our children.

We faithfully ask you, holy Father, on behalf of our fathers and mothers, brothers and sisters, friends and relatives, acquaintances and strangers: Graciously come to their aid when and where they most need it. Amen.

TRAIN UP A CHILD IN THE WAY HE SHOULD GO:
AND WHEN HE IS OLD,
HE WILL NOT DEPART FROM IT.

Proverbs 22:6

WE ASK YOU, HOLY FATHER, FOR ALL THE nations of the world, for kings and all rulers: Give them wisdom and knowledge that they may rule their people in peace, protect and defend the pious, and prevent evil. Do this so they may execute the office and duty that you have assigned to them.

We ask you, holy Father, to give us grace that we may live a pious, God-fearing life under them, able to walk the path of wisdom and truth. May our kindness be made known to all people as we live peacefully and uprightly among them. Amen.

I EXHORT THEREFORE, THAT., FIRST OF ALL,
SUPPLICATIONS, PRAYERS, INTERCESSIONS, AND
GIVING OF THANKS, BE MADE FOR ALL MEN; FOR
KINGS, AND FOR ALL THAT ARE IN AUTHORITY;
THAT WE MAY LEAD A QUIET AND PEACEABLE LIFE
IN ALL GODLINESS AND HONESTY.

1 Timothy 2:1–2

Prayers
of Submission

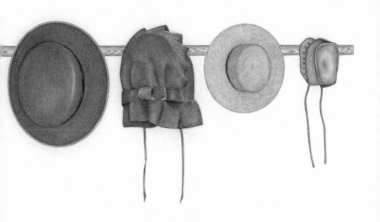

O LORD, ALMIGHTY GOD, HOLY, HEAVENLY Father, you are indivisible, eternal, all-powerful, and you live and reign from eternity to eternity. We come before you, bending the knees of our hearts. We pray that you would bestow your mercy on us, that you would purify our mouths, tongues, lips, and above all our hands and hearts. May we be worthy to call out your great and holy name to praise and thank you. Amen.

AND HE LAID IT UPON MY MOUTH, AND SAID, LO, THIS HATH TOUCHED THY LIPS; AND THINE INIQUITY IS TAKEN AWAY, AND THY SIN PURGED.

Isaiah 6:7

LET YOUR NAME BE GREAT IN ALL THE earth, glorious Lord, so that you may be praised in heaven. Babes and little children speak your praise, for you destroy the enemy as well as the avenger. You are fairer than all humankind, O Lord Christ. Your lips are gracious, which is why God blesses you forever. Amen.

AND BLESSED BE HIS GLORIOUS NAME FOR EVER:
AND LET THE WHOLE EARTH BE FILLED WITH HIS
GLORY. AMEN, AND AMEN.

Psalm 72:19

IRD YOUR SWORD TO YOUR SIDE, O Hero, and clothe yourself in splendor; so arrayed you must succeed. Fight on the side of truth and bring justice to the miserable. For your right hand will do wonders and your arrows are so sharp that even kings among your enemies will fall before you. Your throne is eternal; the scepter of your kingdom is straight and true. You love righteousness and hate wickedness; therefore you, above all of your companions, have been anointed with the oil of joy. Amen.

BLESS THE LORD, O MY SOUL. O LORD MY GOD,
THOU ART VERY GREAT; THOU ART CLOTHED
WITH HONOUR AND MAJESTY.

Psalm 104:1

Lord of Hosts is your name, great in counsel and in deed. Your eyes see all humankind. You are everywhere; you fill heaven and earth. You are infinite. You see, hear, and rule everything and support it all with your strong Word. Amen.

Am I a God at hand, saith the Lord, and not a God afar off? Can any hide himself in secret places that I shall not see him? saith the Lord. Do not I fill heaven and earth? saith the Lord.

Jeremiah 23:23–24

LORD, ALMIGHTY GOD, HOLY, HEAVENLY Father; you are our Creator, Redeemer, Preserver, and Provider. Do not merely provide for our temporal needs, but give us true, living bread from heaven so that our souls will be fed for eternal life.

We do not live on bread alone, but rather—according to the witness of your dear Son, Jesus Christ—on every word that comes out of your mouth. Amen.

BOTH RICHES AND HONOUR COME OF THEE, AND
THOU REIGNEST OVER ALL; AND IN THINE HAND IS
POWER AND MIGHT; AND IN THINE HAND IT IS TO
MAKE GREAT, AND TO GIVE STRENGTH UNTO ALL.

1 Chronicles 29:12

ONCE WE HAVE SURRENDERED OURSELVES and called on your holy name, heavenly Father, look upon us with a benevolent eye, incline your ears to us, and open your gentle hand. Give us clean, obedient hearts, O God and Father, so we might lift them up to you in heaven, where our Savior and Redeemer, Jesus Christ, your dear Son, sits at your right hand. He justified us and ascended into heaven, where we cannot yet follow Him as long as we are bound to the earth. But He has comforted us and promised us that if we ask you, Father, for something in His name, you will grant it and give it to us. Amen.

AND WHATSOEVER YE SHALL ASK IN MY NAME,
THAT WILL I DO, THAT THE FATHER MAY BE
GLORIFIED IN THE SON.

John 14:13

ECAUSE WE UNDERSTAND OUR POWER-lessness and our emptiness, we come before you and ask, dear Father, that you instill a sure, constant, and firm trust in our hearts so that we may hear and grasp your truth. Keep us immovable, as you promised to do through your Son. Declare this truth in our hearts, O Lord. Strengthen our faith so that we may understand how much you love the human race, to whom you are inclined to give good gifts. May we also firmly trust in your omnipotence and know that you do not promise anything, O God, that you cannot readily accomplish. Because you desire what is best for us still more than we ourselves do, let us not see our own unworthiness, but rather your goodness, truth, and omnipotence. Amen.

OH HOW GREAT IS THY GOODNESS, WHICH THOU HAST LAID UP FOR THEM THAT FEAR THEE; WHICH THOU HAST WROUGHT FOR THEM THAT TRUST IN THEE BEFORE THE SONS OF MEN!

Psalm 31:19

ONLY YOU, O GOD, ARE WISE. YOU NOT only dwell in the light but are yourself the eternal Light. Enlighten us who live blind in this dark world with your divine wisdom, which guides us to your throne. Send it from your holy heaven, from your glorious throne, that it may be with us and work in us, and that we may know what is pleasing to you. For without this gift, O God, we do not please you. O Lord, we ask for this wisdom in the name of your beloved Son, Jesus Christ, in whom are hidden all treasures of wisdom and knowledge. Amen.

THE ENTRANCE OF THY WORDS GIVETH LIGHT; IT
GIVETH UNDERSTANDING UNTO THE SIMPLE.

Psalm 119:130

Prayers
in the Evening

WE ASK, HOLY FATHER, THAT WE MAY spend this coming night—which you have ordained for our rest—and all the remainder of our lives under your divine protection and shield. For the powers of darkness and the evil, cunning tempter continually stalk us day and night, seeking to destroy our souls. O holy Father, mercifully protect and defend us from treachery and temptation, and cover us with the wings of your compassion. Amen.

HOW EXCELLENT IS THY LOVINGKINDNESS, O GOD! THEREFORE THE CHILDREN OF MEN PUT THEIR TRUST UNDER THE SHADOW OF THY WINGS.

Psalm 36:7

We ask you, holy Father: Let our bodies rest peacefully, without spiritual or physical defilement, according to your holy and divine will. Let our hearts, minds, and senses remain forever awake in you so that we may be ready for the arrival of your dear Son. Let us prepare thus for your divine direction, and may we await your glorious future with joy. Amen.

And now, little children, abide in him; that, when he shall appear, we may have confidence, and not be ashamed before him at his coming.

1 John 2:28

DEAR MERCIFUL, HEAVENLY FATHER, YOU let us enjoy the clear light of the sun this day so that we would walk faithfully, according to your divine will. We thank your holy name and ask that you forgive us for what we have neglected, and for acting contrary to your will, something we readily confess. Give us grace so that we may lie down to rest in the shadow of your wings of divine grace. May we always be prepared for the return of your beloved Son, through whom we pour out this prayer to you: Our Father, which art in heaven, hallowed be thy name. Thy kingdom come, thy will be done in earth, as it is in heaven. Give us this day our daily bread. And forgive us our debts, as we forgive our debtors. And lead us not into temptation, but deliver us from evil: For thine is the kingdom, and the power, and the glory, forever. Amen.

YET THE LORD WILL COMMAND HIS
LOVINGKINDNESS IN THE DAYTIME, AND IN THE
NIGHT HIS SONG SHALL BE WITH ME, AND MY
PRAYER UNTO THE GOD OF MY LIFE.

Psalm 42:8